The Energy Contest

Laura Townsend
Illustrated by L.S. Pierce

Harcourt Achieve

Rigby • Saxon • Steck-Vaughn

www.HarcourtAchieve.com
1.800.531.5015

Mr. Lawrence opened the window shades of his classroom and looked outside. "The sun is shining!" he said. "It's a perfect day to begin our solar energy unit of study."

"What's solar energy?" asked Frank.

"Solar energy is power that comes from the sun," Mr. Lawrence said. "We will learn that we can use solar energy to do many things."

"It's getting warm in here," Sara said. "May I pull down the window shade?"

Mr. Lawrence said, "Solar energy really heats up the room, doesn't it?"

Mr. Lawrence showed a picture of a house. He said that the black rectangles on the roof were solar panels. He also said that some people use solar panels to heat their houses. "This solar panel is a box with a glass or plastic cover. A fan blows air into the box. Then the sun heats the air, and the warm air heats the house."

After the students learned about ways to use solar energy, Mr. Lawrence told them about a contest they would have. Students would work in groups to study ways people use solar energy and then tell the class about one of the ways.

The contest was going to be outside on the next Wednesday. The class would decide which group had shared the most interesting way to use solar energy.

Soon the whole class was searching for ideas. One group learned that farmers need solar energy so their crops can grow. Another group read about cars that use solar energy instead of gas.

Catalina's group found an idea on the Internet. "We can make a hot dog cooker and use the sun to cook hot dogs!" Catalina said.

Marco wrote a list of everything they needed.

On the day before the contest, Catalina and her group had everything they needed except for a piece of cork.

"The picture shows that we need a piece of cork so the hanger doesn't move," said Marco.

"Let's use an eraser instead of the cork," said Frank.

While Marco got the wire coat hanger ready, Catalina cut the box, Frank found an eraser, and Sara measured the foil.

Soon they put together all the parts. The group was ready for the contest.

The next day, the groups set up their projects outside. Catalina's group put the cooker in the sun so that the light and heat would cook the hot dogs.

Sara finished their poster, and Frank set a timer, while Catalina and Marco cooked the beef hot dogs.

After 35 minutes, Catalina saw steam rising from the foil. It was time for her group to show how their cooker used solar energy.

Hot dogs in cooker

Cooker in sun

Turning hot dogs

The group told the class how the hot dog cooker worked. Catalina explained how the foil kept the sun's heat in the cooker so that the hot dogs cooked faster. Sara said that the wire hanger turned the hot dogs so that they cooked all the way around.

Then Marco took the hot dogs out of the cooker. Frank cut them into pieces so that everyone could taste them.

After the other groups shared their projects, Mr. Lawrence pointed to each group while the class voted.

Catalina's group won the contest, and Mr. Lawrence gave each of them sunglasses as prizes. Then the class stayed outside and enjoyed the sun for a few minutes.

"Learning about solar energy is great, isn't it?" asked Mr. Lawrence.